The Shape of Our Land

by Ann Rossi

Editorial Offices: Glenview, Illinois • Parsippany, New Jersey • New York, New York

Sales Offices: Needham, Massachusetts • Duluth, Georgia • Glenview, Illinois
Coppell, Texas • Sacramento, California • Mesa, Arizona

Dramatic rock formations such as this are common in many parts of the Southwest.

The Different Areas of the United States

The United States is composed of many different regions. Some people divide the United States into the following regions: Northeast, Southeast, Midwest, Southwest, and West. Each **region** has its own unique features. Say "Midwest" to someone and he or she often thinks of a **prairie** stretching toward the horizons. When people think of the Southwest, they might picture a **desert** or dramatic rock formations. The combination of landforms in each region helps make that region unique.

Although each region has distinct features, it may also have a type of **landform** that exists in other regions. Almost every region has a **mountain** range. Regions across the United States have many different landforms. This book will explore some of the varied landforms of the United States.

Regions of the United States

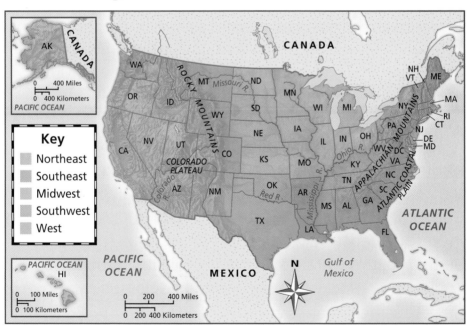

This map shows the five regions of the United States.

Mount Elbert, Colorado, is the tallest peak in the Rocky Mountains.

Mountains and Volcanoes

Mountains are landforms that usually have steep slopes and sharp or slightly rounded peaks. Forces deep within Earth cause mountains to form. Other natural forces, such as **erosion** caused by wind and rain shape them.

The Rocky Mountains are more than 3,000 miles (4,800 kilometers) long and stretch from New Mexico in the Southwest up to Alaska in the West, passing through Canada on the way. They are the largest mountain system in North America. Several smaller mountain ranges make up this vast mountain system. The highest mountain peaks in the Rocky Mountains are in Colorado, where numerous peaks are more than 14,000 feet (4,267 meters) high.

The Cascade Range is another of the many mountain ranges in the West. It is part of the Pacific mountain system that runs parallel to the Pacific coasts in California, Oregon, and Washington for thousands of miles. The Sierra Nevada is part of the Cascades. This range is in eastern California.

Most of the peaks that are part of the Cascade Range are volcanoes. Many are dormant, or have not erupted for a long time. Mount St. Helens, however, is at times active. This **volcano** erupted violently in 1980 after being dormant for more than 120 years. After a period of activity, the volcano again lay dormant. Mount St. Helens erupted again in October 2004.

Hawaii Volcanoes National Park

Visitors to Hawaii Volcanoes National Park can view Kilauea (key-law-WAY-aw), one of Earth's most active volcanoes. Kilauea has been erupting fairly steadily since 1983.

Mount St. Helens is located in Washington.

Inside a Volcano

Ash cloud

Lava
Feeder pipe
Magma chamber

A volcano may erupt when magma, or melted rock, gathers underground in a magma chamber. Pressure from within Earth forces the magma upward through the feeder pipe. The volcano then erupts, spewing out lava and clouds of steam, ash, and gases. *Lava* is the term for magma that erupts onto Earth's surface.

Like the Rocky Mountains, the Appalachian Mountains are part of a large mountain system in North America. Unlike the Rockies, they are in the eastern part of continent, stretching for about 1,500 miles (2,400 kilometers) from Alabama in the Southeast up through the Northeast and into Canada.

Although the Rocky Mountains are the largest mountain system in North America, the Appalachians are the oldest. They are made up of several mountain ranges, including the White Mountains, the Green Mountains, the Catskills in the Northeast, and the Black Mountains and the Great Smoky Mountains in the Southeast. The tallest peak of the Appalachians is Mount Mitchell. It measures 6,684 feet high (2,037 meters).

Mount Mitchell is located in the Black Mountains.

Plains

A **plain** is a large area of flat or fairly flat land. Plains are part of several regions of the United States. The Atlantic Coastal Plain lies along the East Coast of the United States. In parts of the Northeast the Atlantic Coastal Plain is fairly narrow, but it widens in the Southeast and covers much of North Carolina, South Carolina, Georgia, and Florida.

In parts of the Southeast, barrier islands lie off the shore of the Atlantic Coastal Plain. In Florida alone barrier islands make up more than seven hundred miles of the coastline and protect the mainland from pounding ocean waves.

The Gulf Coastal Plain curves along the Gulf of Mexico from Florida to southern Texas. Both the Gulf Coastal Plain and the Atlantic Coastal Plain have many **wetlands**, including swamps and marshes. Rivers flow from inland areas through the coastal plains to the ocean water. Along the way the rivers pick up soil and then deposit it in the low-lying plains, making coastal soils richer.

A prairie is a fairly flat plain covered mainly by tall grasses. Prairies stretch across the Midwest and south into Texas.

Different types of grasses grow in different parts of the rich prairie soil. The types of grasses that grow in the wetter, eastern parts of the prairie grow taller than the grasses that grow in the drier, western part. In the eastern parts of the prairie are grasses that grow more than 6 feet (1.8 meters) high, whereas in the drier western area, the grasses grow only about 2 feet (61 centimeters) high.

The Great Plains is a dry grassland in North America that stretches from Texas and New Mexico north into Canada.

The Mississippi River is a busy waterway.

Bodies of Water

The Mississippi River is the largest river in North America. The Mississippi River begins in Minnesota and travels south. It forms the border between several states in the Midwest and in the Southeast before reaching the Gulf of Mexico. Along the way the Missouri and Ohio Rivers feed into the Mississippi River, making it an important **waterway** in the United States.

Although the Rio Grande's source is in Colorado, it is an important river used to irrigate, or bring water to, crops in the dry Southwest. The Rio Grande flows through New Mexico and forms the border between Texas and Mexico.

Another major river in the United States is the Colorado River. It, too, begins in Colorado. It then cuts through southern Utah and flows into Arizona before forming the border between Arizona and California. Like the Rio Grande, the waters of the Colorado are used to irrigate part of the dry Southwest, but it is also an important source of water for southern California.

The Rio Grande begins in the West and flows to the Southwest.

Rivers are one important kind of waterway and lakes are another. The Great Lakes are a chain of five lakes in the northern United States. Four of the lakes form part of the border between the United States and Canada. Sheets of moving ice called **glaciers** created these lakes long ago.

The lakes are part of a major waterway that connects the Midwest with other areas. For example, the Great Lakes could be part of a boat's route from the St. Louis River in Minnesota to the Atlantic Ocean.

The Great Lakes

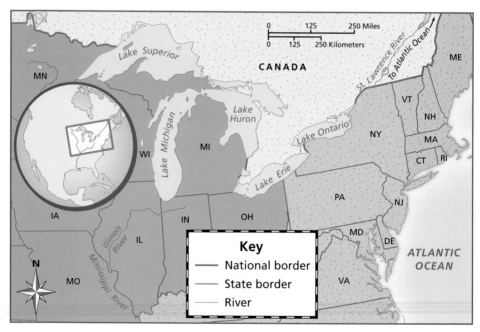

The Great Lakes, rivers, and canals combine to form a network of waterways.

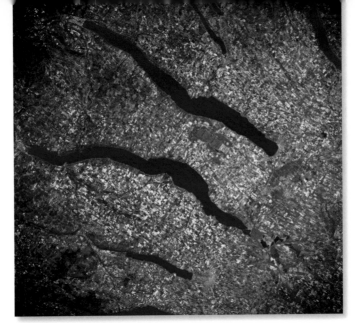

The Finger Lakes in New York State as seen from above almost look like fingers on a hand.

The Finger Lakes are much smaller than the Great Lakes. Unlike the Great Lakes, the Finger Lakes are not linked. Long ago the Finger Lakes were actually rivers. Sheets of ice then reshaped the earth, cutting deep holes in the river valleys and creating the Finger Lakes.

Bottomless Lakes

There are few natural lakes in New Mexico, but the Bottomless Lakes are well known. The greenish-blue color of the lakes makes them appear bottomless, but they really range in depth from 17 feet to 90 feet.

The Mojave Desert is part of the North American Desert.

Deserts

Unlike lakes, which are wet, deserts are dry. In the United States, deserts are located in the West and Southwest regions. The Mojave (moe-HA-vee) Desert in southeastern California and parts of Nevada, Arizona, and Utah is part of a larger desert area called the North American Desert. Although the Mojave is extremely dry—getting only 2 to 6 inches (50 to 150 millimeters) of rain each year, the weather is not always hot. Frost occurs in the winter.

Long ago the Pacific Ocean covered the Mojave Desert. The soil is sandy, and extinct volcanoes are some of the landforms in this area.

All these landforms and waterways—deserts, volcanoes, rivers, lakes, mountains, plains, islands, and wetlands—are just a small number of the extensive natural features that are found in the varied regions of the United States. From the mountain peaks to the coastal plains, they are part of what shape the United States.

The Atlantic Coastal Plain is located on the East Coast.

Glossary

desert an area that gets very little rain

erosion the wearing away of rock by water and wind

glacier huge sheets of ice that cover land

landform a natural feature of the earth's surface

mountain a very high landform, often with steep sides

plain an area of flat land that often is covered with grass or trees

prairie an area where grasses grow well, but trees are rare

region an area in which places share similar characteristics

volcano a mountain with an opening through which ash, gas, and lava are forced

waterway a system of rivers, lakes, and canals through which ships travel

wetland land that is covered with water at times